INTRODUCING WEAVING

INTRODUCING WEAVING

PHYL SHILLINGLAW

B T BATSFORD LIMITED   LONDON
WATSON GUPTILL PUBLICATIONS   NEW YORK

First published 1972
ISBN 0 7134 2431 1
Library of Congress Catalog Card Number 74–188304
ISBN (USA) 8230 6343 7

Filmset by
Keyspools Limited, Golborne, Lancashire
Printed and bound in Great Britain by
C. Tinling and Company Limited, Prescot, Lancashire
for the Publishers
B T Batsford Limited
4 Fitzhardinge Street London W1 and
Watson–Guptill Publications
165 West 46th Street New York NY 10036

CONTENTS

ACKNOWLEDGMENT

I am grateful to the many people who have contributed in any way to this book, especially to Alan Gentle of Rolle College of Further Education, Exmouth, for his many photographs; to Nicholas Horne of Totnes for his photographs of work done by Claire Ash; to Brian Beale of Exeter for his photographs of waist weaving and the use of the pick-up stick; and to Gwen Jackson of the art department of Rolle College for her line drawings.

School photographs were taken at Dr Radcliffe's School, Steeple Ashton, Oxford, Brixington County Primary School, Exmouth, and the many examples of my own students' work from Rolle College.

I would also like to thank my friend Lucile Clarkson for her help and Thelma M. Nye, craft editor of Batsfords for her patient guidance.

INTRODUCTION

The aim of this book is to help those teachers and student teachers who wish to introduce weaving in schools. It sets out in clear, simple stages the process of weaving from the preparation of fibres to the creation of fabrics on different looms.

Various applications of weaving to other subjects are outlined for the teacher who wishes to introduce or pursue further studies.

The sources of raw materials (sheep rearing for wool, flax growing for linen, silk worms for silk, etc), the type of clothing required in different climates, the regions where particular raw materials are cultivated, the production of man-made fibres and the making up of natural ones are subjects which tie in easily with classroom trials with fibres and carding and spinning wool.

The use of vegetable dyes offers an introduction to the science of colour. The process of obtaining dyes from flowers, lichens, berries, etc, and examining the colour of natural objects have obvious application to nature study.

Pattern making requires a basic understanding of good proportion and colour combinations as well as inspiration for design. The making of patterns is based on arithmetical calculations.

The etymology of words in common use which have come from weaving terms and the many references to weaving in Greek mythology, the Bible, poetry and literature can open up a fascinating study.

Many more applications will occur to every teacher; it will be found that teaching weaving to children will open up wider interests and involve other subjects quite naturally during lessons.

CHAPTER ONE

Handling fibres

The basic introduction of any craft to children is the handling of the raw material involved. Children are very sensitive to touch and this is certainly to be encouraged.

Much can be learnt from handling various fibres and trying out their possibilities.

The teacher should have available as many different types of raw fibres as possible. It is important to let the children become thoroughly acquainted with fibres by touch as well as sight. Suggest that they shut their eyes and try identifying different fibres by feel only. Make groups of differing fibres such as wool, fleece, raw silk, bols of cotton, flax, nylon, acrylic fibre (*Courtelle*), polyester fibre (*Terylene, Dacron, Orlon*). Fray out a length of rope made of hemp (coarse flax). This exploratory game will probably be sufficient for one lesson.

For the next lesson get together a wide variety of spun threads of these fibres. Include all types of thick and thin threads (natural and brightly coloured) and compare them with the original raw fibres. This will lead on to vegetable dyeing and the controlled use of chemical dyes.

Trials with fibres

Having accumulated a quantity of vegetable dyed fleece (see chapter two) it will then need to be carded in order to fluff up the fibre and make it look attractive. The colours will be greatly enhanced by placing each pile of carded fleece on to pieces of black paper.

Allow the children to become familiar with this process (see chapter three). The older ones could card the fleece for the younger ones.

Suggested uses for the coloured fleece

One group of students found the making of butterflies an exciting proposition. We visited a nearby museum so that we could see the enormous range of enchanting colours to be found in butterflies from all parts of the world. We studied shapes and made sketches for further reference, either making colour notes or using chalks to aid our memories.

On return to the class room we made enlarged drawings of various butterfly shapes on thin cardboard. This outline was now ready to be filled in with areas of carded, coloured fleece. The fleece was glued down lightly with adhesive and outlined with coloured or black thread. Some were crossed with finer threads taken through the cardboard with a needle and knotted behind. For the bodies a length of black pipe cleaner was chosen. Some students bound parts of the body with coloured yarn. Then the finished shape was cut out. Figure 1.

Making flower heads

Flower heads are a fruitful source of design, both natural and stylised forms.

By treating these in the same way as butterflies, they could well be combined with them to make a large frieze, possibly adding felt leaves, etc. Every child's work could be incorporated, mounted on hessian, and the finished product shown in a school corridor.

Making decorative panels, animal and abstract

Another group of students found interest in the possibilities of using threads and fleece to make decorative panels.

Pieces 254 mm × 203 mm (10 in. × 8 in.) of grey-green hessian were mounted on cardboard. The hessian was wrapped around the cardboard, and both ends were

1   Butterfly made with dyed fleece

2 Animal panel made with dyed
fleece and yarn against hessian background

3 Animal panel filled in with yarn
and dyed fleece

4 Abstract designs using hessian stretched on frames for background

5 A large, decorative panel, outlined with cane and cord, filled in with thick thread and various lichens; flower heads made from fluffed out lengths of binder twine

Plate 1
Design based on a butterfly sketched at a local museum. The original drawing was enlarged and transferred to stiff paper. The coloured areas were filled in with vegetable-dyed fleece and glued in position. Before cutting out the design an outline thread was added.

The body consists of a short length of a fluffy pipe-cleaner

secured at one side of the mount with *Sellotape* (*Scotch tape*).

For these designs the students used their animal drawings made at the museum.

The outline of the silhouette was made with thread (2-ply carpet wool), glued in place, filling in areas such as lions' heads and manes etc with fleece. Figures 2 and 3.

Other students preferred to build up abstract designs on hessian covered boards. Figures 4 and 5.

Experimenting with spun fibres

Have available as many different types of threads as can be mustered. Odd lengths of wool, cotton threads, thick and thin fancy yarns, cord, string, nylon thread, raffia, garden twine, etc. Begin by using only white, off-white and natural coloured threads. In this way, the difference in the fibres will be more easily appreciated by the children.

All the threads can be used for contrast. Threads can be twisted together, knotted at intervals, plaited (braided), or crochetted into a thick chain. Let the children choose a collection of contrasting threads which appeal to them.

Experiment in pattern making with short lengths of threads crossed, entwined, etc, on previously painted postcards. Threads can be held down in ways best suited to the worker, probably most easily held with strips of *Sellotape* (*Scotch tape*) at the back of the postcard.

If working with young children, the teacher might prepare their first cards for them by attaching a variety of threads at one end in a random order and allowing the child to experiment with various arrangements until a good effect is achieved. This would bring the child's attention to the intrinsic nature of each fibre, especially if, as suggested, whites and natural shades are used. It is essential to use coloured cardboard, either previously painted by each child

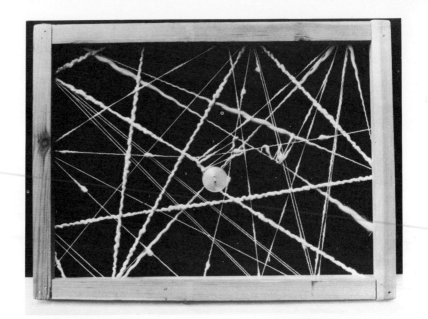

6 An experiment with various
threads, button added as focal point

7 Crossed threads make decorative hoops

(not necessarily of one flat shade as merging colours could be effective) or already coloured cardboard cut into pieces of suitable size.

This preliminary exercise would lead to further experiment with the use of a wooden frame to make a larger thread construction. A frame can easily be made by nailing 20 mm × 20 mm ($\frac{3}{4}$ in. × $\frac{3}{4}$ in.) wood into a square or rectangle. Deeper frames offer more possibilities for use as they allow threads to cross in depth, giving a three dimensional effect.

Simple weaving or entwining of threads would be possible here, especially for older children able to use weaving needles, ie, bodkins with turned up points, or, for young children, needles made from lolly pop or ice cream sticks with an eye pierced at one end.

Threads may be held in position with drawing pins (thumbtacks). Obviously, only a soft wood should be used for the frames or there will be difficulty in pushing in the drawing pins. Figure 6.

Another idea used was the crossing of coloured threads on children's wooden hoops borrowed from the gym. Figure 7. These make very decorative circles and would be an excellent teaching aid by using coloured threads to divide the circles into halves, quarters, etc.

The above few ideas will inspire a class to take its experiments further. Figures 8 to 13.

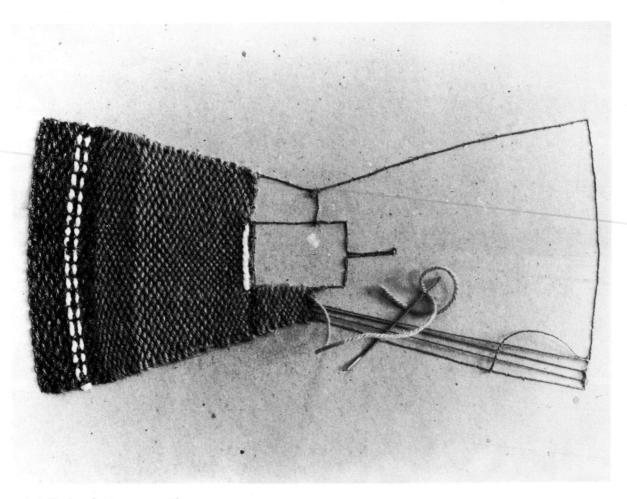

8   A doll's dress being woven with
a bodkin, using an outline thread
tacked down to cardboard

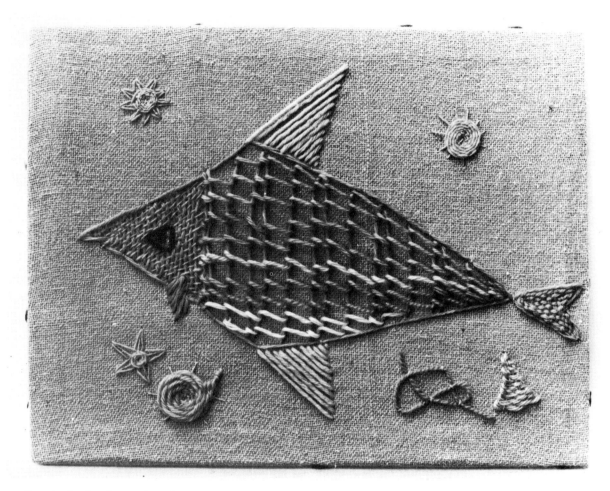

9 Practice in simple weaving, the
outline thread tacked down on a
piece of hessian to hold the warp
and weft

10 Lampshades can be made by winding threads such as string, cotton, raffia, raffine, etc around ready-made frames which come in a variety of shapes and sizes

Above right
11 An exploratory exercise in enclosing space with fibres, using

12 dampened cane held in place by a lump of clay

13 Animal made from binder
twine, black cotton and red felt,
legs stiffened with glue. A series of
different animals mounted on a turn
table, suggesting a fair ground
might be made

14 Junior children tend their sheep
at Dr Radcliffe's C of E Primary
School, Steeple Ashton, Oxford

CHAPTER TWO

Dyeing

Vegetable dyeing should be mainly confined to fleece (ie, unspun wool), or already spun wool (yarn), as this is by far the easiest fibre to dye. Figure 14.

Some form of heating is a necessity, together with several small enamel saucepans for experimenting with the dye stuffs, many of which may be brought in by the children themselves. Figure 15.

It will be necessary to use a mordant to ensure permanency of results. Powdered alum (obtainable from most chemists (drug-stores) in *small* quantities, if wished), together with the dye stuff in the same pan will produce satisfactory results for colour experiments.

The amount of mordant required is 113 g alum to 454 g wool, roughly equivalent to 1 teaspoonful of alum to 28 g wool, which may be a simpler and more practical measure to use in the class-room. Keep to alum mordant for use with small children as it is non-poisonous. Other mordants, such as tin crystals, are poisonous and should not be used until they are thoroughly understood by both children and teacher.

The amount of gathered dye stuff required is usually reckoned as weight for weight, ie 28 g wool to 28 g dye stuff.

Dissolve the requisite amount of alum in warm water in a saucepan, add the dye stuff, covering well with more warm water, put in a sample of fleece or yarn and bring the con-tents of the pan slowly to just below boiling point. Simmer for not less than 15 minutes, or 30 minutes for deeper shade.

15 Vegetable dyeing by pupils at
Brixington CP School, Exmouth

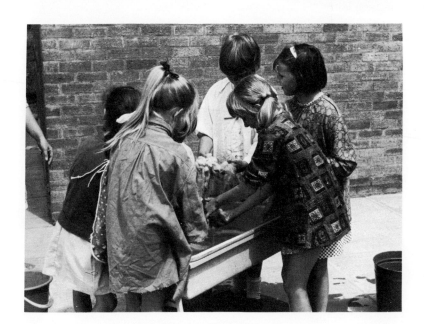

16 Rinsing the fleece after dyeing,
Brixington CP School, Exmouth

The longer the fleece or wool is simmered, the deeper the colour. Similarly, increasing the amount of dye stuff will give a deeper shade.

When dyeing is completed, lift out fleece with a wooden spoon, rinse in warm water and allow to dry. Figure 16.

There are many easily found plants which will yield colour, eg flower heads, leaves, stalks and roots, barks and lichens. These can be brought in by the children and tried out.

Yellows, oranges, greens, fawns and browns are the colours most easily obtained from nettles, roots, stems and onions skins, and in Great Britain from gorse (a favourite in the West Country), bracken tops and heather tips. One student got a lovely flame colour from corn-marigolds and a similar shade from dahlia heads.

Onion skins yield an excellent pale yellow down to deep orange. Only the outer brown skins should be used as these will leave no odour in the dyed wool. This dye stuff is always available in children's homes. Suggest keeping *only* the outer brown skins. A clean cocoa tin or unwanted glass jar with a tightly fitting lid are both suitable for storing. So stored, the skins can be kept until wanted, age, within reason, not mattering.

Other types of mordants can be used to get different shades from one dye, or even different colours, but it should be stressed that teachers should study them before deciding on the suitability of their use by the age group with which they are working.

The teacher who decides to experiment further would be well advised to mordant a lot of wool in advance and keep the mordanted wool in well labelled polythene (poly-ethylene) bags for use when wanted. The wool should be dried before storing in the bags unless intended for im-mediate use. Such treated samples could be put together in one dye bath by the children and the different results noted.

Here is a list of the most common types of mordants with the amounts to be used:

Alum	113 g to 454 g wool
Bichromate of potash	14 g to 454 g wool
Tin crystals	7 g to 454 g wool
Copperas	14 g to 454 g wool
Cream of tartar	28 g to 454 g wool

(may be used to brighten colours)

Lichens give a chance for much research as they are available in many areas. Those growing on outcrops of granite yield excellent results. Lichens do not necessarily need a mordant, but it helps the dye run more easily. Any of the mordants mentioned above can be used.

The feathery fronds hanging from old trees give beautiful shades of yellow, beige, etc.

If tap water is the only supply available use a few drops of ammonia to help soften the water; care should be taken to keep the bottle strictly out of the reach of children.

It is always of interest to the dyer to put small samples of different fibres into each dye bath and note and tabulate the effect according to mordant used, dye stuff, time of year gathered, length of time dyed, etc. Each child should be encouraged to keep a folder of his own notes. Keeping a separate card for each experiment, with mounted samples of dyed fibre, date and notes as above can be invaluable for future reference. One college (high school) student experimenting for her final study had annotated some 400 samples of vegetable dyes.

CHAPTER THREE

Carding

For first rate spinning it is necessary to prepare fleece by carding. Figures 17 to 19.

Only a small quantity of fleece should be spread on the left hand carder which should then be well stroked with the carder held in the right hand. To finish, roll up carded fleece by reversing direction of carders and make into a neat roll for spinning by placing it on the back of one carder and rolling it with the back of the other. This roll is called a *rolag* by spinners. Primary school children are well able to sort out and card fleece, as shown by photographs from both Brixington School and Steeple Ashton School. Figures 20 to 32.

17 The carding process: a layer of fleece is put on the left hand carder

18 The fleece is well stroked with the carder held in the right hand

19 Carded fleece is rolled up by reversing direction of carders, making a *rolag*, fleece ready for spinning

20   Wool sorting, Brixington CP
School, Exmouth

21   Teasing fleece, Steeple Ashton, Oxford

Plate 2
A group of hand-spun and vegetable dyed skeins of wool. Many dyestuffs have been used including

lichens giving a range of yellows, oranges and browns
iris flower heads giving a green
cochineal making reds and pinks, and when crossed with
logwood giving mauves and purples
fustic chips making yellows
madder giving an indian red
indigo and *logwood* giving blues

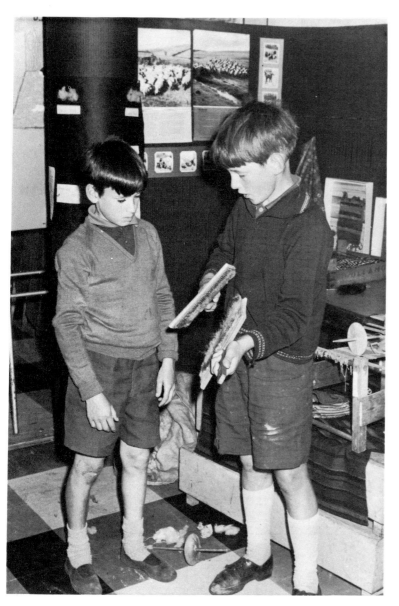

22 Teaching the carding process,
Steeple Ashton, Oxford

Making a spindle

These small pieces of spinning equipment are inexpensive and easy to make. If preferred, spindles can be bought. Any child able to use a penknife can make a workable spindle in half an hour. A number of spindles using dowel rod or bamboo for the shaft and circular rubber heels for the whorls were made in the class-room.

Many museums are good hunting grounds for finding decorative whorls of bone, clay, stone and wood made by our early ancestors.

Spindle spinning

1   The spindle must first be prepared by tying on a piece of already spun wool (2 or 3 ply knitting wool is suitable). Approximately 508 mm (20 in.) will be required.

Tie one end of the wool just above the whorl, take over whorl and catch it around the point of the shaft, making a half hitch knot around the notch. Leave a length of the spun wool free. Figure 23.

2   At this stage, let the children hold the prepared spindle suspended in the left hand, rotating the now dangling spindle clockwise with the right hand, giving the top of the shaft a sharp twist.

3   Having carded or simply teased a handful of fleece (ie, pulled apart the fibres to let any foreign bodies, such as leaves and twigs, fall away), pull out one end of the fleece and place it between the untwisted end of the spun wool already on the spindle. Allow the wool and fleece to twist together, making a join.

4   Hold fleece in the palm of the left hand, rotate spindle shaft with right hand, and the twisting fleece will be felt to be making a yarn. Keep control of the spin with the left hand finger and thumb so that the twist is neither too tight nor too hard.

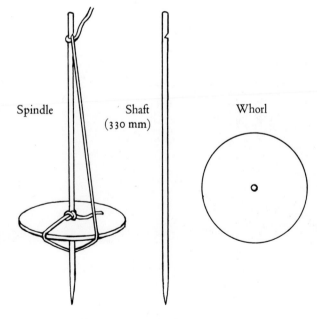

Spindle   Shaft
(330 mm)

Whorl

23   A spindle, shaft and whorl

Continue to pull out fibres from the fleece with the right hand until the spindle reaches the floor.

5 When control of fleece and spindle is gained and a length of yarn is achieved, unhitch wool at spindle shaft notch and wind yarn around the shaft in a figure eight, leaving about 508 mm (20 in.) to set up spindle as originally shown.

Small children seem able to spin at once if shown this process, as they are able to by-pass the analytical process which besets adults. Certainly the majority of my own students were able to spin at their first lesson. Figures 24 to 26.

Note that the fleece is best spun in its original oily condition. If washed first it is then necessary to add oil to the fleece.

24 Spindle spinning with unwashed, carded wool, Steeple Ashton, Oxford

25 More spindle spinning,
Brixington, Exmouth.
Note fluffy join

26 A child's impression of wheel spinning after visiting author's studio

CHAPTER FOUR

Weaving   The interlacing of threads is the basis of all weaving. The crossing of threads at right angles forms the web of the material.

Warp   The long threads which are held taut on the loom.

Weft   The interlacing or crossing threads.

Loom   Any device which keeps the warp threads stretched. Many of the beautiful Peruvian textiles of long ago were woven on the simplest looms, as a study of craft history will show. Therefore, a lack of complicated equipment should not bar the production of excellent work.

Looms for beginners should be of the simplest variety. Several differing types, and their uses are described:

Frame looms

Frame looms as originally designed by Miss Elsie Davenport are excellent. The warp can be quickly set up for any type of material to be woven, and, as the whole warp is visible, its possibilities can be easily assessed.

Their use is much to be preferred to card looms. A child can use his fingers on a frame loom; this is better than using a weaving needle which a card loom requires. No tool should be used until it is grasped that the tool is an extension of the hand.

These frames are easily made as shown in figure 27. The size of these looms can vary considerably, as the principle of construction is the same. If the loom is too small, it will restrict the work; however, mats for a doll's house, for example, could well be made on quite small looms.

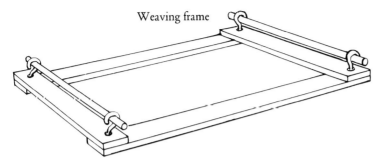

Weaving frame

27   A frame loom

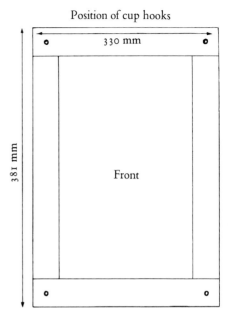

Position of cup hooks

330 mm

381 mm

Front

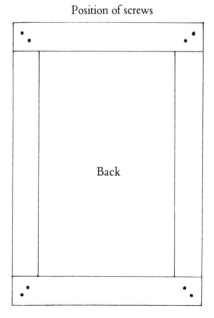

Position of screws

Back

Photograph 28 shows a frame warped up with twine and ready to use. A piece of twine twice the length of the frame, plus enough left for tying, has been looped around the top dowel rod, brought down and taken over the lower rod. One end of the twine has been brought up on either side of the double warp thread and tied securely. This warping action is repeated across the width of the frame.

Thick rug wool would be an excellent thread for beginners' use. Figures 29 to 31.

When warp is completed, the frame loom is ready for weaving. The weft may be threaded over one (doubled) warp thread and under the next. Repeat this action across the width of the frame, pressing each row well down. For small fingers short lengths of weft should be used at first, the ends left to form a fringe.

If a different colour weft from the warp is used, this in itself will make an interesting contrast. Eventually, the class should experiment with unusual threads and colours to achieve exciting effects.

Quite pleasant small mats can be made from first efforts, and many interesting articles are possible on these simple frames, such as table mats, shoulder bags, hot water bottle covers, to suggest only a few.

28 Home-made frame loom, warp
of twine, set up, ready for use

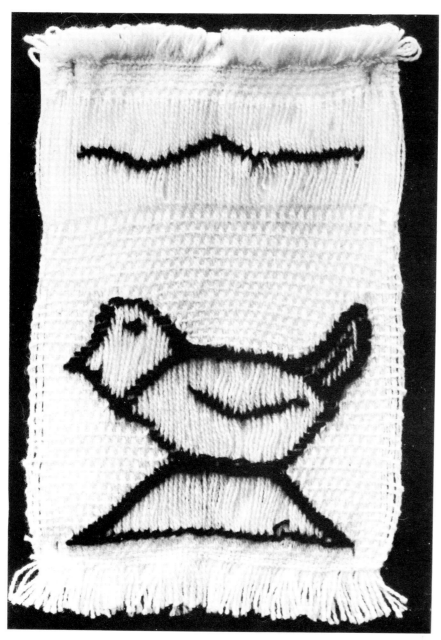

29 On plain weave background, soumak stitch bird, woven on frame loom. Note unwoven warp

30 An exercise in counting warp
(four black, four white) and
experimenting with weft picks,
altering numbers to build up
patterns, woven on a frame loom

31 On a frame loom a
decorative fish form is woven,
copied from a museum specimen

32 Stick shuttle

33 First trials with small looms,
Brixington CP School, Exmouth.
Note use of stick shuttle

The rigid heddle

This is a clever device which makes it easier to lift the warp threads and to bring the weft across the warp in one action. This process is greatly helped by using a stick shuttle. Wind the weft thread lengthways around the shuttle which has two convenient grooves to hold the threads. Figures 32 and 33. The stick shuttle enables the weaver to use a continuous weft thread.

The parting of the layer of threads made by using a rigid heddle is called by weavers the shed. A rigid heddle consists of a length of smooth metal with alternate slits and eyes. Figures 34 and 35. Hook the first warp thread (single) through an eye, the second thread through a slit. Repeat

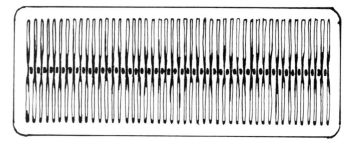

34   A rigid heddle

35   Absorbed weavers, Steeple Ashton, Oxford. Note rigid heddle in use

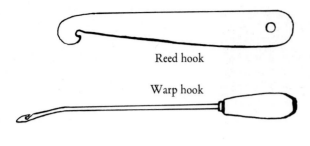

Reed hook

Warp hook

36   Warp hook

this action with all the warp threads across the width of the frame loom, using a warp hook. Figure 36. When this process is completed, raise the rigid heddle to use the shed, ie the opening between the two layers of warp threads. The weft thread can now be passed across the warp in one action. On its return journey, depress the rigid heddle so that the weft can pass over the threads previously passed under.

The basic principle of plain weaving is now understandable as over one thread and under the next. Each weft row is called a pick and each warp thread an end.

Once the use of a rigid heddle is grasped the way lies open for many adventures in the making of materials. It certainly speeds up production. Figure 37.

If it is desired to use a rigid heddle with the frame loom, ascertain sizes available and suit loom measurements to them. (Note that the rigid heddle will need freedom in which to move.)

Waist weaving

With a rigid heddle it is also possible to dispense with a loom. Having cut lengths of warp threads (making a generous extra allowance on the desired length), thread them through the rigid heddle as already explained. Gather up one end of the warp threads and tie them securely to a fixed object. Tie the other end of the warp to a stick, which should then be secured around the waist of the weaver. The tension of the warp is kept by the weaver's position. It is now possible to proceed to weave, using a stick shuttle. Each row must be pressed towards the weaver with a stick or ruler.

Scarves and belts are suggested articles which may be woven this way. Figures 38 to 40.

37 Shoulder bag made with
vegetable dyed carpet wool as weft
and a string warp, made on a frame
loom using a rigid heddle

38 Waist weaving a belt, using a small rigid heddle. Note method of rolling and tying up

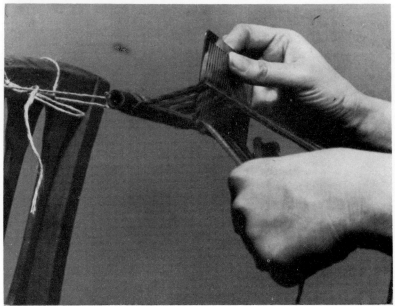

39 Belt nearing completion

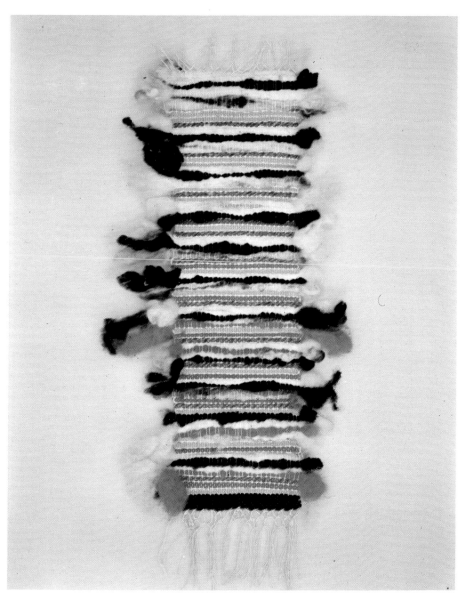

Plate 3
A first piece of weaving by Claire Ash when she was twelve years old. The materials are mainly unspun vegetable-dyed fleece, with some spun wool. Note the pleasing contrast between the two textures

40 Scarf and trial piece for belt,
waist woven with rigid heddle

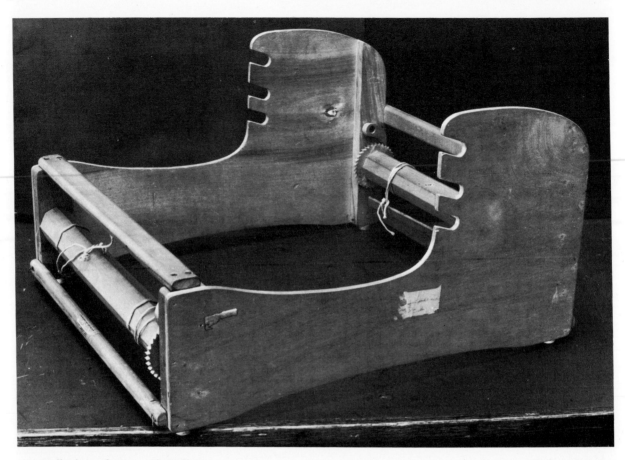

41 Roller loom for use with rigid
heddle. Note sockets to hold
framed heddle supplied with this
type of loom

Roller looms with rigid heddles

Having used the frame looms it will be evident that only
a certain length of warp is a possibility, determined by the
length of the frame. The next stage is to grasp the idea of a
roller loom which offers greater flexibility. These rollers
are fitted to either end of a deeper frame which allows room
for the turning of the warp threads at one end and the
rolling on of the woven fabric at the other. Thus, a longer
length of material is possible. Figure 41.

To make a warp 2 m (6 ft 6 in.) long or longer it is necessary to use a device to hold this continuous warp. Two useful methods, warping posts and a warping board, are illustrated. Figure 42. Study this figure well, especially noting how the threads cross, making a figure eight. This is most important, for it keeps the order of the threads. When winding is completed, tie up the cross (ie each bundle of

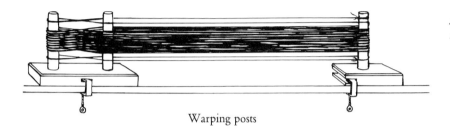

Warping posts

42 Warping posts and a warping board

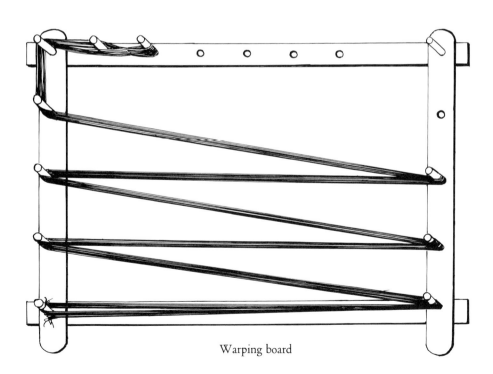

Warping board

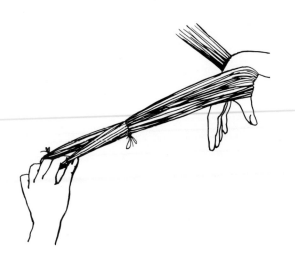

threads), separately. Next, chain up this warp as shown in figure 43, beginning at the end without the cross. Thread a pair of cross sticks through the already tied up bundles and secure sticks together, as shown, before releasing threads from tied up cross. Figure 44.

Spread out warp loops held by cross sticks and hook one loop (one loop represents two threads) through each slit in the rigid heddle. As each loop is hooked through, thread loop on the rod which has been cut to the width of the loom. When all loops are so threaded, tie this stick onto the back roller (the roller furthest away from you). At this stage, the warp should be spread out to the width required and attached by the looped stick to the back roller. Proceed to wind on the warp evenly, keeping it taut, until most of the warp is wound on, leaving enough out to tie to the front roller.

It is a good idea to wind in brown paper together with the warp to make the threads lie evenly. Figure 45. Pull tight on warp while winding to keep an even tension.

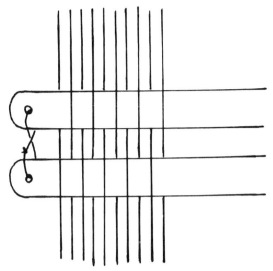

44   Secure sticks together. Note method of tying

45   Small roller loom made by a student. Note use of paper wound in with warp

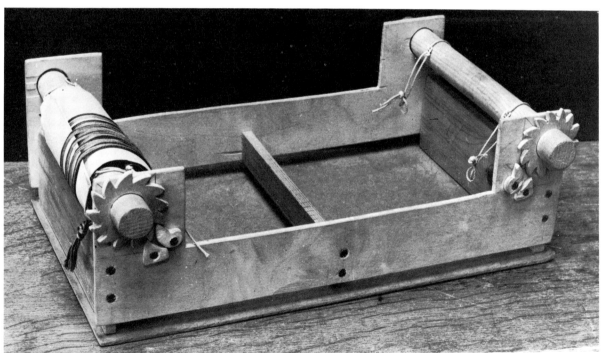

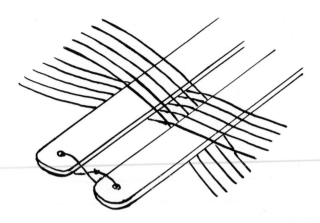

46 The right order of threads as shown by the cross sticks

The pair of cross sticks must now be put on the other side of the rigid heddle. Take care to keep them in the same relative position. Having done this, cut the end of the warp, which will leave two single threads through each slit. Pull out one of these threads from behind the rigid heddle and replace it in adjacent eye, taking great care to keep the right order of threads as shown by the cross sticks. Figure 46. To tie up take four threads over stick attached to the front roller, divide and cross underneath, bringing up two threads from either side of the group of four threads and tie securely on top of these four threads. Repeat this across warp, test for even tension, adjusting where necessary. The loom is now dressed and ready for weaving.

Having once grasped the principle of setting up these simple roller looms, the dressing of a 4-shaft table loom will present no problem at a later stage; it will be seen as a logical sequence.

So much can be done with these roller looms, using a rigid heddle, that it will be found possible to continue their use for a long time without exhausting the possibilities. Figure 47.

Colour, texture and pattern

These can be explored. A few suggestions follow:

Colour
a   warp=blue
    weft =red
    result shot purple

b   warp=2 ends blue, 2 ends white
    weft =2 picks blue, 2 picks white
    result small check

c   warp=irregular stripes
    weft =one colour only
    result muted stripes

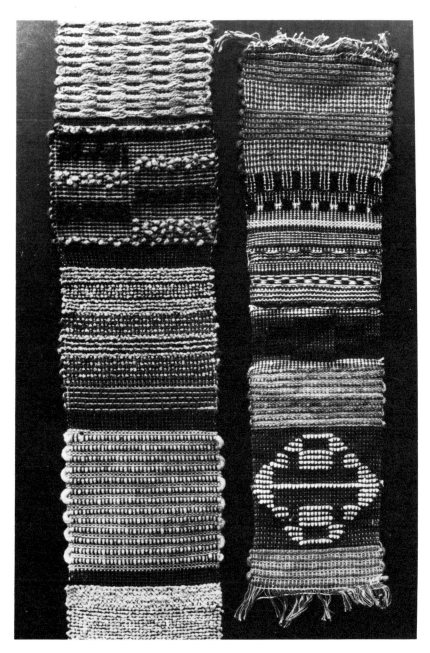

47 Samplers showing some
possible effects using a rigid heddle
roller loom

d warp=25 mm (1 in.) each of red and yellow
   weft =25 mm (1 in.) each of red and yellow
   result red, orange and yellow squares

Texture

a warp=thick threads alternating with thin
   weft =the same as warp

b warp=all plain cotton
   weft =1 pick gimp (or other fancy yarn)   3 picks
            plain cotton

c warp=2 ends thick cotton
            1 end thin cotton
            1 end gimp (or other fancy yarn)
   weft =the same as warp

d warp=string
   weft =1 pick cane, 3 picks string

48 Pick-up stick (ruler) when not in use (pushed well back)

Pattern

It is possible to make very interesting patterns by inserting a stick (known as a *pick-up stick*) behind the rigid heddle, picking up certain of the warp threads which are in the slits. When this *pick-up stick* is turned on its side and brought up near the rigid heddle, it will make another shed. Figures 48 to 50. When not in use, push stick well back or it will make the weaving difficult. When using this extra shed, always follow with an uneven number of plain picks; one or three picks are usual. If this is not done the weaving will become too open. As the weaving progresses, it is essential that each row should be well pressed down, using the rigid heddle as a tool to do this beating. It will be found that there is a certain take up of the weft as it interlaces with the warp. To allow for this, each pick should not be pulled too tight. Practice will quickly show the beginner how much to allow.

Cushion covers, sets of place mats and narrow width skirt materials can be woven on these simple roller looms. Many children find this an incentive to produce good practical work. The addition of the *pick-up stick*, as described, allows great freedom in design. Figures 51 and 52.

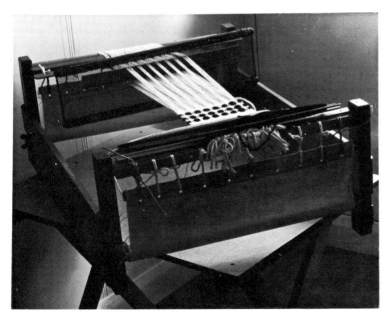

50 Pick-up stick close to rigid heddle to give a good shed through which to pass a shuttle

51 Interesting weaves on a rigid heddle roller loom using a pick-up stick

52 Rigid heddle loom free shuttle weave with pick-up stick. Embroidered leaf shape added for extra interest

Two shaft roller looms

These looms introduce the raising of alternate threads by using shafts, or heddle, frames, on which string or metal heddles are suspended. These shafts have a raising method, either with levers or cords.

The heddles have eye-holes in the middle through which the warp end is hooked before finally passing through the reed.

The reed is a length of flat metal the width of the loom, having a specified number of slits or dents in it. The purpose of the reed is to keep the warp ends in position as each thread is threaded through its appropriate dent. The reed is held in a wooden frame which works on a swivel enabling it to act as a beater. A reed hook or a warp hook are useful for threading reeds. Figure 36 page 42.

It will be realised that the rigid heddle has now been super-seded by a heddle frame, or shaft, and a reed. The purpose of this loom development is to make possible any desired number of warp threads to 25 mm (1 in.) (referred to as EPI or ends per inch (25 mm), and, also, to make it easier to lift these warp threads by means of a raising device, thus greatly speeding up the weaving. Reeds differ in the number of slits or dents to 25 mm (1 in.); an 8 dent reed is a useful number and preferable to a 14 dent, the one usually supplied unless requirement is specified with order.

At this stage introduce simple pattern drafting. This is the weaver's shorthand for all *warp threading*. It is written on squared (graph) paper for easy reading. For two shaft looms, it is a simple plan to be read from right to left. Each black square represents one warp thread and shows the order of threading. The two lines enclosing the black, or white, squares represent the two frames. The frame, or shaft, nearest to the weaver is No. 1.

It is now clear that the first warp end is hooked through the first heddle on shaft 2, the second end on shaft 1. This is repeated across the whole width of the warp.

All warp threads should be thought of in pairs as the weft thread must go over one and under one warp thread to weave the web of the material. Figures 53 to 55.

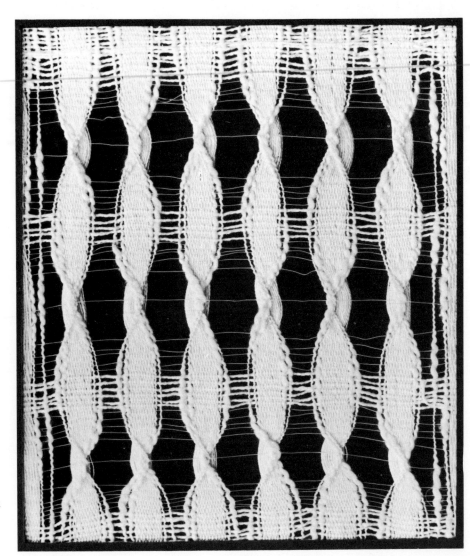

53 Exciting possibilities of open weave. Twisting of warp threads (leno) to form shapes could be woven on a 2 shaft loom

54 Meeting and parting technique, using three shuttles, woven on a 2 shaft table loom

55 An unspun fleece rug woven on a 2 shaft table loom, one row of knots followed by six rows of slightly twisted fleece. Knots should not be taken right up to selvedges on either side

Four shaft table looms

These looms have an additional 2 shafts, making more intricate patterns possible. Figures 56 to 60.

Start with the simplest threading which is a straightforward 4—3—2—1.

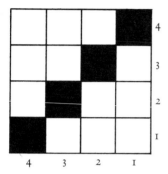

The shaft raising order can vary considerably. For plain, or tabby, weaving raise shafts 1 and 3 together (the uneven numbers) and shafts 2 and 4 for the next row (the even numbers).

When the tabby weaving is grasped, let the children experiment with shaft raising so that they will understand exactly what happens. If shaft 1 is raised, it will be seen that the weft thread will pass under one warp thread and over three. If this is followed by raising each shaft in turn for one pick and this sequence repeated, a three and one twill will be produced. If, for example, a white warp is put on and a black weft is used, the material (if well beaten during the weaving), will result in material mainly black on the top side—and mainly white on the under side.

When first setting up the looms, always begin by using a thick thread. This makes for clarity in seeing just what happens to both warp and weft threads. Figures 61 to 64.

56 Harris model 4 shaft table loom.
Note method of shaft raising

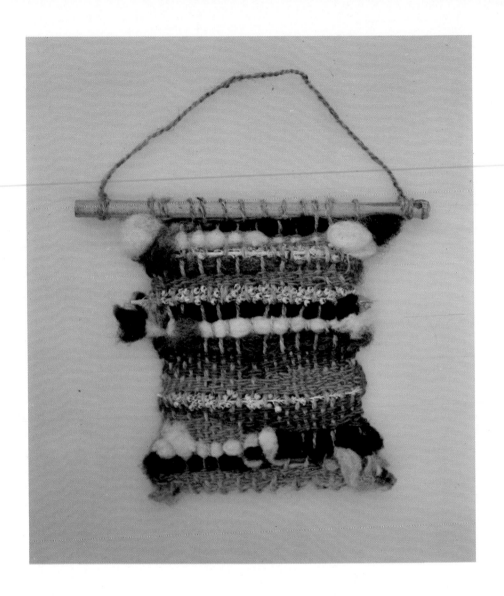

Plate 4
A hanging by Claire Ash. This small piece included some natural dried plants which had been picked up whilst on holiday in Corsica and Sardinia. This example shows an excellent awareness of differing materials

57 A work exploring the use of tapestry weave, derived from Peruvian work woven on an open background, woven on a 4 shaft table loom. Stones are used to weight warp ends

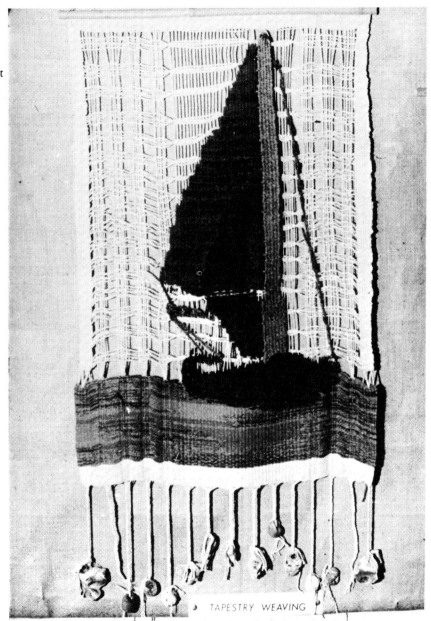

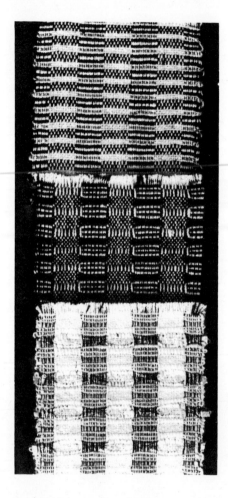

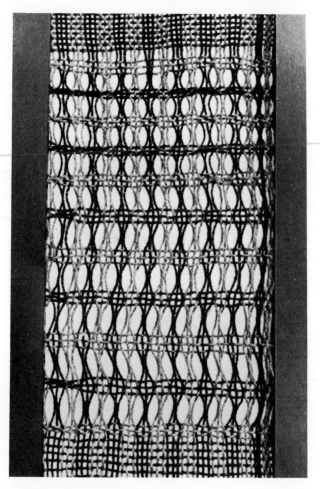

58 Samples to show development possible on the same threading draft, woven on a 4 shaft table loom

59 Use of horse hair, cow hair and monofil to make this open but tough fabric, woven on a 4 shaft table loom

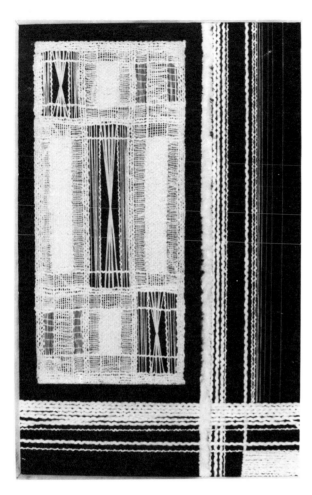

60 Woven panel made on a 4 shaft table loom combined with stretched threads mounted on black card and framed. Panel was designed by a third year student

61 Hand woven background and applique pieces, stitchery added in the needlework department. Could be woven on 2 shafts

62   Skirts woven by students on 4
shaft table looms

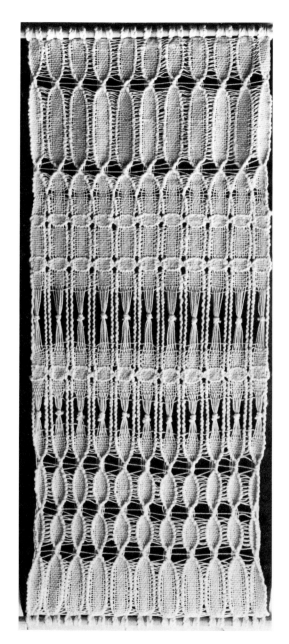

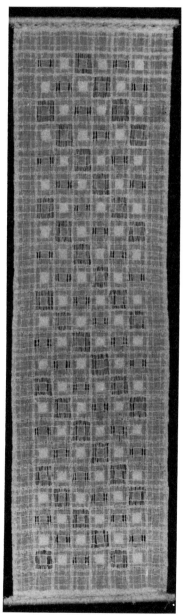

63 Various warp twistings make up this wall hanging, woven on a 4 shaft table loom with off-whites and natural coloured threads

64 An intricate design woven by a third year student on a 4 shaft table loom

Rug frames

Uncomplicated rugs can well be woven on a suitable size frame loom. (Figures 65 to 67.) The warp should be made of strong twine, 3 doubles to 1 inch. For the weft use either 6 ply rug wool or, preferably, three strands of 2 ply rug wool. The latter gives more scope for colour blending. Three different blues, for example, used together in this way will produce a very lively result.

See photographs 68, 69, 70 and 71 for the effects of different methods of rug weaving. Photographs 54 and 55 are also possible to make on a rug frame.

Whichever method of rug weaving is used, the simpler the design the better it will look on the floor. Let the material, colour and proportion speak for themselves.

65   Rug frame, designed and made by Dr C W Chapman. Note device for tensioning

66 Rug weaving: A first sampler, woven on a picture frame with staples top and bottom. Note: one pick red, one pick black results in upright bars of colour; two picks white, two picks black results in crossways stripes. At top of sampler the meeting and parting technique is used

67. Clever device for making it possible to use 4 shaft weaves, when attached to a rug frame. Designed and made by Dr C W Chapman

Weaving terms

A considerable number of weaving terms have been introduced, particularly in this chapter, and are defined in the glossary. It is a good idea for children to write their own list of weaving terms for future reference. A word quiz can help to fix terms in their minds.

68   Section of a tapestry woven rug,
made with natural coloured wools,
fawn, brown and black. Woven on
a 4 shaft foot loom, using 2 shafts

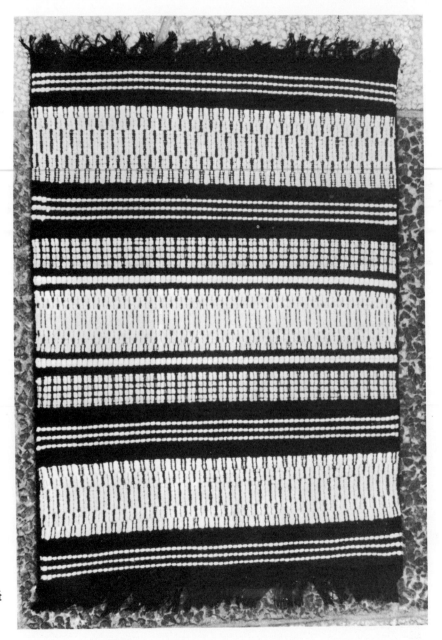

69 A bath mat woven on a 4 shaft
table loom, using plain cotton and
cotton gimp

70   Woven on a 4 shaft table loom

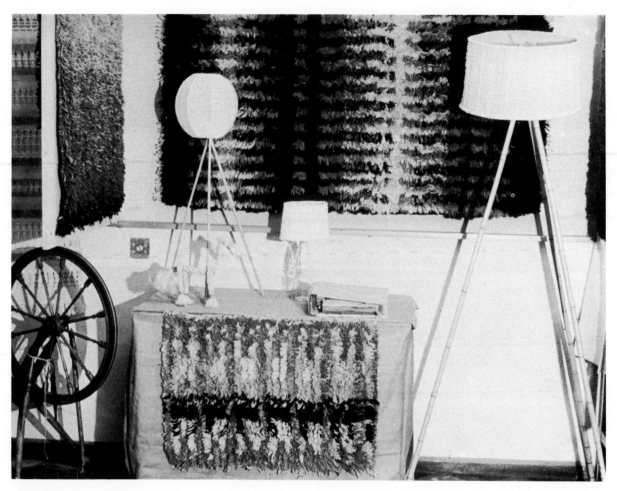

71　Lampshades and rugs woven
by students, on display at end of
weaving course

GLOSSARY

Beam   A roller or bar across the loom.

Beaming   Rolling the warp onto the back roller or beam.

Beater   A device for pressing down rows of weft threads.

Beating   The pressing down of rows of weft when weaving.

Carders   A pair of rectangular pieces of curved wood with handle, having bent wire teeth on one side.

Card loom   A length of cardboard notched at both ends to hold warp threads.

Chain   One loop inserted through another.

Chain up   The making of a continuous chain to safeguard a prepared warp.

Cross   A bundle of warp threads crossed in a figure eight to keep them in order.

Cross sticks   Sticks placed through the cross to retain it.

Dent   The space between two wires on a reed.

Dowel rod   A length of rounded stick.

Dressing the loom   The processes of making the loom ready for weaving.

End   A warp thread.

Ends per inch   Any number of warp threads per inch (EPI). A standard unit.

Eyes   The openings in the rigid heddle, alternating with the slits, through which one layer of warp threads are threaded.

Heddle   A loop made either of metal or string with central eye through which the warp ends are threaded, and by which they are raised or lowered.

Loop   A doubled length of thread.

Pattern drafting   A diagrammatic plan for warp threading.

Pick   One row of weft.

Pick-up stick   A length of thin wood such as a ruler, used for making an extra shed in weaving.

Reed   A piece of flat metal the width of the loom for keeping the warp ends in position and beating the weft.

Reed hook   A fine, flat hook for threading the reed.

Rigid heddle   A heddle made of a length of smooth metal having alternate slits and eyes through which alternate warp ends are threaded.

Rolag   A roll of carded fleece ready for spinning.

Roller   See beam.

Shaft   The frame on which heddles are threaded top and bottom.

Shed   The opening between two layers of warp ends.

Slits   The openings in the rigid heddle, alternating with the eyes, through which one layer of warp threads are threaded.

Spindle shaft   The rod in a spindle used for twisting and winding the thread in spinning.

Spreading   The arranging of warp threads to the desired width on loom.

Stick shuttle   A rectangular slat of wood notched at either end to hold weft thread.

Tabby   Plain weave.

Teasing   The process of pulling fibres apart.

Tie up   The method of tying up warp ends to the front beam on a loom.

Twill   A cloth construction in which the weft threads move so as to produce a diagonal effect.

Warp   The long threads which are held taut on the loom.

Warp hook   A fine, small hook set in a wooden handle for threading heddles.

Warp sticks   Smooth wooden slats placed between rows of warp threads as warp is being wound onto back beam.

Warping board   A board or frame set with pegs around which the warp is wound.

Weave   The interlacing of ends and picks.

Web   The cloth on the loom.

Weft   The interlacing or crossing threads on the cloth.

Whorl   The disk threaded onto the spindle shaft.

UK SUPPLIERS

Equipment

Looms and Reeds, rigid heddles and small equipment
Dryads, Northgates, Leicester

Harris Looms, North Grove Road, Hawkhurst, Kent

"Atlas" Handicrafts, Manchester, 4

Looms and reeds
The Hand Loom Centre, 59 Crest View Drive, Petts Wood, Kent

Spindles
Dryads, Northgates, Leicester

Hand-made spindles
Richard Dell, Craft Centre, Teignmouth, Devon

Dyes and Mordants
Comak Chemicals, Swinton Works, 11 Moon Street, London, N.1

Materials

Tweed wools
T. M. Hunter, Sutherland Mill, Brora, Scotland

Rug wools 6 ply and 2 ply and warp twine
Weavers' Shop, Royal Wilton Carpet Factory, Wilton, Wilts

Mohair, chenilles, gimps, worsted
J. Hyslop Bathgate and Co, Victoria Works, Galashiels,
Scotland

Cotton, hemp, jute
Southwick and Case, 89–91 Prescot Street, Liverpool, 7

Very good special yarns
Hugh Griffiths, Brook Dale, Beckington, Bath, Somerset

Cottons—by return post
The Hand Loom Weavers, Fourways, Rockford, Ring-
wood, Hants

Top quality natural, wools, fleece, warp flax
Craftsman's Mark Ltd, 36 Shortheath Road, Farnham,
Surrey

Odd lots

All types. Inexpensive yarns. Quick service
A. K. Graupner, Corner House, Valley Road, Bradford,
B.D.1 4 A A

Good illustrated leaflets on setting up looms are obtainable from

Dryads, Northgates, Leicester

Leaflet No 91—*Hand-weaving on Two-way Looms*
Leaflet No 89—*Hand-weaving on Four-way Table Looms*
Also
Handloom weaving, *Atlas* Leaflet No 62. *Atlas* Handi-
crafts, Manchester, 4

Excellent carders
Miss K. R. Drummond, 30 Hart Grove, Ealing Common,
London, W.5

US SUPPLIERS

(courtesy American Crafts Council 29 West 53 Street New York N Y)

Manufacturers of looms

Bexel Handlooms 2470 Dixie Highway, Pontiac, Michigan

Gilmore Looms, 1032 North Broadway Avenue, Stockton, California 95205

Herald Looms, Bailey Manufacturing Company, 118 Lee Street, Lodi, Ohio 44254

LeClerc Industries PO Box 267, Champlain, New York, *or* 195 Rue Sauve Est, Montreal 12, Canada

L W Macomber, 166 Essex Street, Saugus, Massachusetts

Looms and equipment can also be obtained from :

Ayotte's Designery, Center Sandwich, New Haven, Connecticut 03227

Edward Bosworth, (handmade looms), 132 Indian Creek Road, Ithaca, New York

Countryside Handweavers, Box 1225, Mission, Kansas 66222

The Craftool Company, 1 Industrial Road, Woodridge, New Jersey 07075

Magnolia Weaving, 2635–29th Avenue, W. Seattle, Washington 98199

New Valley Handweaving Service, PO Box 76, Pinedale, California 93650

Robin and Russ Handweavers, 533 North Adams Street, McMinnville, Oregon

Ross Hill Handweavers, 102 West Court Street, Ithaca, New York 14850

School Products Company, 312 East 23 Street, New York, New York 10010

The Silver Shuttle, 1301 35th N.W., Washington, D.C.

Threads : Wools, yarns, flax, etc

Briggs and Little Woollen Mills, (yarn, rug wool, and wool), Harvey Station, New Brunswick, Canada

Contessa Yarns, (yarn and carpet wool), PO Box 37, Lebanon, Connecticut 06249

Countryside Handweavers, (handspun yarn and synthetic dyes), Box 1225, Mission, Kansas 66222

Craft Yarns of Rhode Island Inc, (yarn and macramé), 603 Mineral Spring Avenue, Pawtucket, Rhode Island 02862

Frederick J Fawcett Inc, (yarn, fine grade linens, macramé), 129 South Street, Boston, Massachusetts

Gary Jones Sheep Farm, (wool), RR 3, Peabody, Kansas

S Achiye Jones, (wool), 2050 Friendly Eugene, Oregon 97405

Magnolia Weaving, (yarn, rug wool, wool, macramé, jute), 2635-29th Avenue, W., Seattle, Washington 98199

Old Mill Yarn, (yarn and rug wool), PO Box 115, Eaton Rapids, Michigan 48827

Paternayan Bros Inc, (high grade rug wool), 312 East 95 Street, New York, New York 10028

The Silver Shuttle, (yarn), 1301 25th N.W., Washington, D.C.

Shuttlecraft, (yarn), PO Box 6041, Providence, Rhode Island

Dyes

Arnold, Hoffman and Co Inc, (procion dyes), 55 Canal Street, Providence, Rhode Island

Ciba Chemical and Dye Co, (synthetic dyes), Fairlawn, New Jersey

Countryside Handweavers, (synthetic dyes), Box 1225, Mission, Kansas 66222

Fezandie and Sperrle, Inc, (synthetic dyes), 103 Lafayette Street, New York, New York 10013

Glen Black, (procion dyes), 1414 Grant Avenue, San Francisco, California

Nature's Herb Company, (vegetable dyes), 281 Ellis Street, San Francisco, California

Putnam Fadeless Dyes Inc, (vegetable dyes), 301 Oak Street, Quincy, Illinois 62301

For further information contact

Research and Education Department, American Crafts Council, 29 West 53 Street, New York, New York